The Bleeding Heart Poet

ALSO BY AHMAD AL-KHATAT

Gas Chamber
Love on the War's Frontline
Wounds from Iraq
Roofs of Dreams

The
Bleeding Heart Poet

poems by
Ahmad Al-Khatat

Poetic Justice Books
Port St. Lucie, Florida

©2017 / 2019 Ahmad Al-Khatat

book design and layout: SpiNDec, Port Saint Lucie, FL
cover image: *De wil van het volk*, mixed media on cardboard, 19 x 27 cm, 2019; Marcel Herms

All rights reserved.

No part of this book may be used or reproduced in any manner whatsoever without written permission except in the case of brief quotations embodied in critical articles and reviews. Members of educational institutions and organizations wishing to photocopy any of the work for classroom use, or authors, artists and publishers who would like to obtain permission for any material in the work, should contact the publisher.

Published by Poetic Justice Books
Port Saint Lucie, Florida
www.poeticjusticebooks.com

ISBN: 978-1-950433-36-0

REVISED SECOND EDITION
10 9 8 7 6 5 4 3 2

*This book is for
everyone who has had a bleeding heart*

contents

Death Is Nothing At All...	3
Ants Curiosity...	4
My Tears...	6
Wrong Sits...	8
Such a Selfish Homeland...	10
Greatest Punishment...	12
Lustful And Sinful...	14
Do Not Go Gentle...	16
Leaves On The Dead Body...	18
Lost...	20
A Low Refugee I Was...	22
Unspeakable Words...	24
We Hate Peace...	26
Life	28
Don't Kiss My Coffin...	30
Love Letter to Noemi...	32
Sunny Moments...	34
I Am...	36
Talking About Noemi...	38
Under The Lights...	40
The Candle...	44
The Sound of Rain...	46
The Cottage of Love...	48
It Ends With You...	50
The Nightingale	52

The
Bleeding Heart Poet

Death Is Nothing At All...

Death is nothing at all
You might be a brother to me
You are unseen friend and
An invisible last guest to visit me

If you will come tonight
You don't need an appointment
I have nothing to gain or lose
But, please come to me quietly

I do not want witnesses
To observe my death
Talk to me when my parents and
My beloved's eyes are well dreaming

I just do not want anyone to
Stand at my grave and weep
Tears are the signs of weakness of
Sinners and my enemies fears

Would you mind allowing me to
Finish my poem about this moment
Since, I cannot cry with tears
When I was blinded from the sunshine

Go into me gently and harmlessly
On my knees, I will pray to God lastly
The clouds will rain and we will walk away
Bloodlessly, without a sound or noise.

Ants Curiosity...

Once there were
Two curious ants

First was curious
About something

Why does everyone
Have a pack back?

Like little children
Parents, grandparents,

Homeless, suiciders
Unemployed workers

Gamers, the doctors
engineers, and alcoholics?

Second replied after
She laughed for a time

Because people are
The smartest kind

For creating silly
Serious decisions
Fail in the real life

They play and
Win to nowhere

They read and
Can't write a word

They love and
Ignore happiness

They hope and
Stop dreaming forever!!!

My Tears...

I can't think about anything else
Except the pain he caused me
my bottle of rum is almost empty I start

Drinking from my bottle to reduce the
Weight of the pain that he caused

Half of the people don't share the same value
Of love that I built with you

A quarter of the romantic couples don't have the same
Feeling that I shared with him every night
he left me alone with tears in my eyes

He was resting in my thoughts and
He was fortunate to be there but

I guess he never realized that
Once my eyes started dropping tears

He became a pain in my thoughts
that won't be easy to forget
my soul loved him more than anybody else

I put him in my arteries only so we could feel each
Others pain and injures and so no one would try to

Take him away from me
but since my eyes started dropping
tears things started looking different

He injured me with my own blood
And my Soul lied to me by adding
him to my blood as a cancer

so I hope my tears will try to make him
Understand that I'm in a lot of pain and
that my soul is still with him

Wrong Sits...

Life has always been the same
With sweet and bitter journey
Four colorful seasons of a year
Rich people smile and poor don't

In the pages of unwritten misery
We read about bloody battles
That destroyed the future joys
Into a bag of dusty skeleton and bones

Nowadays, we choose wrong sits
We sit in the wheelchairs of soldiers
And throw them in the dirtiest corners
To be the miserable slaves for low income

We hate the beautiful moments of the day
We open wounds and bleed like a raining cloud
And never heal ourselves, waiting to close
Our eyes and stop our hearts from beating normally

We cross illegally into the ethical standards
Fleshes have no more private parts to be hidden
We exposed shamelessly to the strangers
Just to buy a few nights of fake lustily and glory

We ran away from dictatorship leaders homeland
So we could have a colorful life and full of blessings
Instead, we embraced the culture of low self esteem
And smoke tobacco and fly by the plants like a crow

We must live, but we must choose to die anyhow
We burned down the photos and videos and paintings
Yet, we tried to extend the clean air to breathe bigger
Therefore, we could avoid depression and love life more

Such a Selfish Homeland...

Such a selfish homeland
I was born and raised in
Very young and I damaged
My childhood for political purposes

Such a selfish homeland
Create emotions lead to arrange
Marriage with husbands die
And wives raise kids to die pricelessly

Such a selfish homeland
With schools and buildings
With unlocked doors bleed
Souls escape from the locked windows

Such a selfish homeland
Parks are full of old tombs
Farmers are planting less than a
Gravedigger digs in a graveyard everyday

Such a selfish homeland
To hear more of crying and
Moaning than a joy of being
Alive between the fire and the fall of blood

Such a selfish homeland
With dreams can't be true
Now there is no reason for
Anyone to hope while we are all drowning in exile

Such a selfish homeland
To wake up under the misery
And hold sorrows deep inside
Drinking liquor and smoking will never be the result

Such a selfish homeland
To hear the echo of death
Calling all the eyes to weep
In all the holidays instead of sharing a good time

Such a selfish homeland
To die the beauty of the seasons
Into a flying leaf to nowhere
And a candle light on for a greater tomorrow

Greatest Punishment…

Falling in love
With you was
My best choice

I am my own
And so you are
It's nobody belongings

Pain and sadness
Are created by me
To miss you always

Love and yearnings
Are greatest punishment
To draw you awake

A strength
I need nowadays
To kiss you in dark

A power
I embrace daily
To cuddle you in day

Those eyes
If they don't cry
I will turn them down

A short story
Was the journey
Now, it's a love song

Let the doves
Fly without wings
Set them to sewing

A peaceful dress
With stones from
The stars and planets

Seven years ago
He was incapable
Of lifting you a bit up

Seven months ago
I am capable to lift
You up to the heaven

Poison me with a look
Die me with a touch
Suffer me with a greatest punishment

Lustful And Sinful...

Your sweet love survives
And mainly surprises me
I am lucky to be in love
Always lustful and sinful

The house of eroticism
I built with all you want
I will turn the lights off
To taste your pure silk

Watching your flesh nude
Turn me into a Parisian lover
Blind about dark and dangerous
And mute to say a single word

Good times bring white stars in
Bad times kick black tears away
I can't believe that I am hot and
The world is weak and I'm hard

I may not be the man with muscles
But I know for a fact that what's up
Front of me counts the most to you
I'd rather give it so you can guide him

A hard man with sweats and emotions
Is good to be able to do so much as I do
While you are licking my skin raw and
Gently till I numb and you start moaning

In my throat, there is a new song for you
Force me singing it to serve you longer
Since your name is written on the water
That is found on the planet I made for us

Do Not Go Gentle...

Do not go gentle into that night
Remember, I am the happiest man
I have been writing about you forever
In the red knights and yellow days

My captain sunk the ship willfully
Just so I can't see my grandpa
Heaven by my grandparents yard
'Fore the angels slaughter my neck

The last letter I haven't seen it yet
Whenever I want to write this letter
A tear ran down my cheeks painfully
I am so not well, but remember me

You took the woman of mine shamelessly
Without the chance to say goodbye honey!
My heart is still with her between healing and
Paradise, while I am still shining like a habit

After great views of dead victims in Iraq
I arose a bitter pain of being an aimless writer
Do not go gentle into the silence of my night
Before the sun heals my sorrows and suffering

Just one thing I should say before I forget
I am the son of Baghdad without memories
I am the happiest friend to wait for you at dawn
Take me now, I am worried if I dream of hopes

Leaves On The Dead Body...

It's not easy to confess or talk
About my melancholy journey
Mainly because it gives me a
Breakdown if I ever mention it

Being down than the sea waves
It's like self drowning in the sea of
Misery and life sentence for sorrows
Unable to smile without serious tears

I met and fell in love with the woman
Who is today my wife for the past years
She was suffering from a low spirit as well
During her youth age but not anymore

As I grew up, I lost control of the right side
Of my body periodically, it may be small strokes
I worked in an office job company was doing well
I was the last hired and first to be let go

Now it's been the sixth month of unemployment
We eat loaves and fishes almost every day
And stretching the money of unemployment cash
Which it can be seen as a heavy load to hold

Nowadays, I spend most of the time my own
With my grandson since my daughter cannot
Afford a daycare for the moments being
Through him, I could smile and laugh out loud

No matter how much I need to find a job
Even though I see this world as leaves on
The dead body of misery and rainless clouds
I am the optimism and my wife is the real one

Her realism had gradually worn into the ground
You may judge me as a homeless or a drunk driver
I really will not be down again when I see the sunshine
Feeling that one day, I will be stronger and healthier

Lost...

I am lost without any knowledge
If I am going to be living in
Another day, another tomorrow

Under the temperature of sorrows
I broke my boundaries and I laughed
With all the blood running waste

I just want to see a sea without the waves
I just want to touch a flame without the fire
I just want to feel better without the drugs

I give my values and faith away
So my friends see my cool temporary
And my mirror sees my unseen regrets

Lovers hid from one corner till they die
Below the candle light and not the moonlight
They don't drink as much I do without you

Such as a miserable man to find myself
Alone in the dark and breathless moments
Unable to control my ink to write beautifully

Such a lucky woman you are now
You drink my unreachable inspiration
And eat my semi damaged heart with a smile

Lucky I am to have another birthday
To live a life without losing in my new dictionary
Without dark lonesome, but happy, to love you

Did you hear me moaning from the locked
Doors and watch the rusty tears on the windows
That was my space in the freedom of depression

Over two hundred contacts and four hundred
Friends in my social networks accounts alone
Big number, but seen as one graveyard with benefits.

A Low Refugee I Was...

Nobody knows about my plans
I am mainly unseen, unheard,
And unfortunately I am the victim

Only 'cause I am not holding a weapon
To fight against darkness and success
Instead, I decide to be a low refugee

I start removing my tiny shelter
To pack up in an old backpack
Like a turtle, below the rain and snow

I smile to the sad laughers' faces
And lie about being well as usual
With tears falling in bad or good moments

With days to go on like a dying wind
So slow that I could feel I am dying but
Sadly, it doesn't like a pen facing a bullet

My heart is already falling in yearnings
With swords around my belly button,
If I ever step back to the miserable past

I have no coins to buy a fancy burger
I only hold the keys of the damaged lock
From my homeland, I will try to eat it

I am preparing a bouquet of thoughts
Some are just autumn branches with thorns
And others are flowers to a Catholic woman

I have secretly planted them in spring
Pouring them with the tears of a good faith
Which I cannot describe how much happier I am

Between her breasts I lay my head down
Feeling the light of love and warm support
A low refugee I was but now I am a loving bird

Flying with broken bones, wings, and almost
Heading towards the gate of the healing process
To smile like the first time I had my first French kiss

Unspeakable Words...

Do you remember me
Or I am mistaken again for years

You were the sugar in the morning
In the cup of warm coffee

And the hospital to my miseries
In the island of eyes don't weep tears

The man who came back to sleep
He forgot to stab me by the dead palms

Our hearts were young and beautiful
When you kissed me like a king of holiday

Make a joyful sound in the stranger house
Perhaps, he would confuse the dark mystery

Send no flowers nor unspeakable words
Just visit me once in a while and remember me

Ahmad Al-Khatat

We Hate Peace...

We hate peace ... We hate peace,
Because peace has been never real in our dark life.

Lots of thousands of papers demanding peace,
Were signed by leaders who fought against it.

Democrats made our Paradise land into a wild
Forest, turns out to be in a civil war country.

Where a brother kills his older brother because
He doesn't want to be a supporter of the leader.

Republicans prayed more than once to Jesus,
Asking forgiveness to create a new deadly war.

In which bullets get to be the bees where
People ran away from them, to protect their kids.

United Nations they have signed over thousands,
And spoke over hours and still united to celebrate the Holocaust.

Since the gold coins were always in their accounts,
None of them care about the numbers of martyrs in

Palestine
Iraq
Syria
Lebanon
Egypt

Sadly those countries where life of Jesus was born and
Died as well, now they are less popular because we

And they wanted to speak out, that we hate peace
So we will create our own plan to have peace back

So little kids go outside and play in the park, like
The birds who play and sing in the blue color sky.

Life

Life still has a meaning
Even though some people
Will hurt you and cause
You pain and suffering

Life has faith and courage
You are born to learn how
To create a mistake and to
Forgive and forget about it

Leave the past behind the scenes
Open the moments into new pages
And create new characters to love
Burn all the negatives with positivity

Life is to failures and success
Both walk in the same sidewalks
You believe in the uplifting path
And I don't believe in my artwork

Help me to be creative like you
Be kind to my mind and I promise
You I will be happy and never sad
So, we will together appreciate life.

Don't Kiss My Coffin...

In times of sorrows
Back in the awful past
I carry mask to hide
My tears from my mirror

I lit all the beauty I own
In seconds without chances
Till, I met with the death
Who wears a beauty mask?

I wore his beauty mask
And I start having small cuts
Losing control of myself
Laughing with bloody tears

Suicidal feelings and thoughts
Were real and never went away
I yelled out till you woke me up
And you embraced me like a soldier

Moments later, the sunshine
Appeared and I told you a secret
Don't kiss my coffin, sweetheart
Sunday, my proses will be rhymes

An unseen spirit trapped in a cage
I was all alone like a fall cloud
Dropping God tears above us
I will fly in the hidden dream.

Love Letter to Noemi...

I love to spend a night by you
Do not ask me why and since when
Perhaps, if you smile to me
I feel like a kid riding a bicycle
With a smile of the size of the sunshine

I even love to see you nervous
Talking like an autumn thunder
And lightning from your two eyes
Dropping shy drops of happy rain
I adore the taste of fruits from your lips

Without you I am a falling tree
With colorful leaves blowing off
Each color describes my state
Surely, only mean and negativity
I need a branch from you to green again

Love cannot live over 365 days
Be the home to my new pages
Be the room to my real emotions
Be and be the guider to my feelings
Born me and die me in your heart

I may fail when it comes to love you
Would you let me weep on the piano
Since my tears could read my love better
Than the self-mirror of the fantasies
Because of you I am a flying bird in your heaven

Sunny Moments…

You look so handsome my friend
Mainly when you are laying down
In this dusty grave from days ago

This life is beautiful 'cause of you
Your mother is dropping shining
Tears like as if they are diamonds

I love the way the doves fly above
Your tomb and sing of the grief
The wind weeps to the clouds to rain

Without you I am a priceless penny
I wish I could have drank of yr blood
To gain the scent of your own courage

Military suit is being suitable on you
With different useless medals on side
I wish that you live again and I die for you

Nightmares and tears are my journeys
Working with low income my life is now
Barely happy but always proud of you

To have you as a friend to miss the most
The rainbow is colourful when he arises by
Your grave in the flying leaves of misery

The bombs and bullets and black smoke
The mindless enemies and dead bodies
Are fading away from the mind and never

You still remain alive with a smile
On the borders between joy and sorrow
Making dark memories into a sunny moment

I Am...

I am brown skin color
I was born with it and
I had no choice to change it
But accept it as I am

My name is familiar to
Certain serial killers
With my age suitable
For a death penalty

I am Arab and friends
With the Africans, the Asians
And with the Spanish
We are truly peaceful

I am Muslim and proud
My neighbor is Jewish
My best friend is Christian
We drop the same salty tears

With my faithful believes
My beloved she is Catholic
We see ourselves in the paradise
Since our hearts are breakable

One black policemen said
You are from a terrorist group
While my homeland fought
And won the battle against Isis

While he forgets about his
Grandparents suffering from
Being the unknown soldiers to
The slavery in the land of freedom

I am always smiling and
Living my day as the last
I may be a nobody with
Bloodless thoughts to share with

No weapons, No white flags
No white doves, but perhaps
I need one widow, and one orphan
To adopt a family to understand

The life of a poet with broken wings
Mainly if it is like me living 'tween all
The strangers with my tears bursting
My heart beats to live another day

to say I am so I am the knight from
Baghdad, not willing to get my hands
With gold coins to fight against anyone
Perhaps, this life still has beautiful eyes

Talking About Noemi...

Not everyone
Could be trusted
Those days
Even if somebody
Try to steal a heart
For a good or bad cause

If the sun shines
And you are not by me
I don't want the day
Nor the moon and stars
All I want is a flower
With a scent of yearnings

Talking about Noemi
It's the most beautiful song
Less than a sentence
One kiss could be
A story about romance
That would drop tears

If you ever meet her
Tell her that I want her
'Fore the alcohol drunk me
In directions leading to
Dark side of the depression
Where I will wish only to die

Lovers usually dream big
While I'm crying over my dreams
I feel so old toward her heart
Unable to find a reason to believe
That I'm going to be a fiancé
And husband and mainly a father

Noemi once told me
You are able to get answers
From all of those faces
While you are a question
With the answer in my spirit
Please, love me and get your answer

By her wonderful families
I feel like a miserable burning candle
Sharing invisible tears of joy
They drank with laughter memories
In the days when I was
Running out with my family to survive

My heart cannot love anymore
My mouth closed from kissing
My breaths are limited to a few days
Will Noemi love me with no worries
Will Noemi kiss me without bleeding
Will Noemi witness my last words

So many thoughts and confusions
It arose me hundred times closer to death
Suffering from the moments of destiny
The birds are singing to my daily aches
And Noemi cuddles with me tightly
To burst my poison into a scent of love

Under The Lights...

Under the sunlight
I walked you
A long way
I talked about
My true love
To you alone

Under the moonlight
I kissed you
For the first time
And tasted
Your lust
From the tongues

Under the starlight
I unlock your bra
Rubber the breasts
With a mouth
Wetting your
Rose leaves

Under the candlelight
I drank a cup
Of white wine
While you were
Already drunk
In love with me

Under the flashlight
My hands
Were naughty
Like a farmer
Cutting the grass
When I was dipping

Under the lamplight
I confessed to you
That you are
More than a friend
Perhaps you
Are my fiancée

Under the firelight
We were by
All our friends
Dancing with me
Laughing from
Your silly tales

Under the twilight
I will be a vampire
Swallowing all of
Your stress and
Anxiety and grief
Till you smile forever

Under the light
Of autumn leaves
I love you maybe

Under the light
Of the summer rain
I love you so so

Under the light
Of the winter falcon
I love you too

Under the light
Of the spring scent
I love you so much

Under the influence of
Your sweet mother
And awesome family
I demand you
If you want to
Have abound with me

The Candle...

I
Once
Told
To the
Burning candles

Remember
The day
When
You
Will die

Lovers
Recall their
Misery
And
Nothing good

Just like
A
Widow
Visiting
the graveyard

Or
Maybe
A bee
Kissing
The flower lips

The Sound of Rain...

Under the sound of rain
I was reading a poetry book
Nearby the sound of laughter
Women swimming in the lake

I refused to swim with them
I didn't have a choice but to read it
Reading some related lyrics
To see the sun hid behind for a bit

And the clouds started dropping
As I'm finding myself weeping
From reading about dark ages
Where I felt lonely and miserable

The sound of rain was too loud
That for once it felt as the clouds
Were shooting me with the bullets
That looked like tears from heaven

The trees wet their own leaves and
Extend to their branches to dry all
The flowers and cut the breath out
So I couldn't remember anyone

Scented that I always miss by nobody
But the rain alone recalled me of my
First time dating the woman I love
Messy hair and thirsty lips to kiss

The Cottage of Love...

In the cottage of love
Next to your nude flesh
My dreams are made

If you say it firstly
Then I am falling for you
With the sweetest touch

Meet me in the lake
So we dance like loons
And talk wordless in a kiss

He wanted you to give him
Chances and dark hopes
While he never appreciates a thing

Seven years and you were
Nobody but a rose in the desert
When I loved you was 'cause

I was missing arose in my life
I grabbed and planted you
Shamelessly in the darkest days

Slowly and surely and soon
I started seeing a smiling angel
I observed him and it was my reborn

Nobody was born to be perfect
And creating mistakes to learn about
Therefore, let's not judge our failures

If you love me like the sea waves
Hide me from the tears of the boat
Let it float in the river of his stupidity

We are not together because we're thirsty
Nor of love story that blows away with
The autumn leaves under the tears of lovers

Come with me and let me draw you alone
Let the sun shine above your nibbles again
To suck them and numbs myself below you

Open your beautiful eyes and guide me
Hold both hands tight and be on the top
Far enough to reach the moon and stars

It Ends With You...

Who will knock on the gate
Of your heart, it's not important

Smile so the route of happiness
Takes more from the sorrows route

This life itself has lots of holes
Filled with gray tears and miserable tales

People are limited characters now
Liars, cheaters, betrayers and soulless

Not judging all the people but those
Clowns are the most common nowadays

Lover lie and drink to forget his funny lies
You ignore and dance to enjoy the moments

I was born under the sweats of serious war
And now I'm fearless if my destiny it's death

Be happy without a benefit to any mankind
It ends with you, but remember you are so

Beautiful...

The Nightingale

Still young with a soul out of my control,
my heart lost his emotional beats.
Feelings the arrival of autumn clouds,
when I am waiting for you in my spring.

I drink my tears and swallow the bitter taste of grief,
pretending to be drunk.
Hiding as much more aches as I can,
when I spent nights like the nightingale.

I sang with my yearning alone to you,
When you are cuddling with the stranger.
I wrote with my emotions just for you,
When you are dancing upon my rhythms.

You were never alone,
I was by your window like the snowflake melting slow.
I was the autumn leaf by your home stairs,
when you throw our pictures away.

I held the microphone and I sang with love,
and start dreaming as we are one.
One heart, one love, one feeling that danced
up high in the bosom of the moon.

Nobody understood my love sad songs,
but the spring flowers felt my pain.
I tried not to weep but I couldn't,
but I did after I read your last honest message.

You left me in darkness, where I spent years
home alone in my own depression.
I drank your poison so I died to the hell,
started suffering of living my life with sins.

Still young I believe I am ready to die anytime,
I failed making women loving me.
A humour like me won't be indeed a grave,
nobody will visit a clown in the graveyard.

Ahmad Al-Khatat was born in Baghdad, Iraq. His work has appeared in print globally and he has poems translated into several languages. He has previously been nominated for the *Best of the Net* awards. He lives in Canada.

www.ingramcontent.com/pod-product-compliance
Lightning Source LLC
Chambersburg PA
CBHW030133100526
44591CB00009B/638